LOOK INTO SPACE

OUR SOLAR SYSTEM

Jon Kirkwood

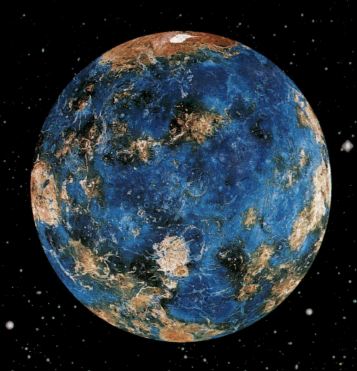

ALADDIN/WATTS
LONDON · SYDNEY

An Aladdin Book
© Aladdin Books Ltd 1998
Produced by
Aladdin Books Ltd
28 Percy Street
London W1P 0LD

First published in Great Britain
in 1998 by
Aladdin Books/Watts Books
96 Leonard Street
London EC2A 4RH

ISBN 0-7496-3383-2

Editor: Jon Richards

Design

David West · CHILDREN'S BOOK DESIGN

Designer: Simon Morse

Illustrator: Ian Thompson

Picture research: Brooks Krikler Research

Printed in Belgium

The author, Jon Kirkwood, is a freelance
author and editor who has written a
number of books for both adults and
children, mainly on astronomy.

CONTENTS

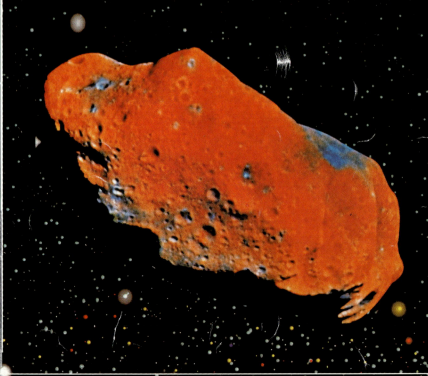

INTRODUCTION

Have you ever wondered what lies in space, beyond the comfort of the Earth? *Our Solar System* will take you

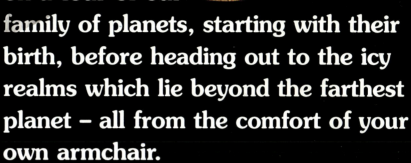

on a tour of our family of planets, starting with their birth, before heading out to the icy realms which lie beyond the farthest planet – all from the comfort of your own armchair.

Practical experiments will help you to discover many facts about the Solar System, without having to leave the planet. These include a rusty key which tells you about the surface of Mars, a floating balloon which shows why the giant planets are so 'light', and what a simple magnet can tell you about lights in the sky.

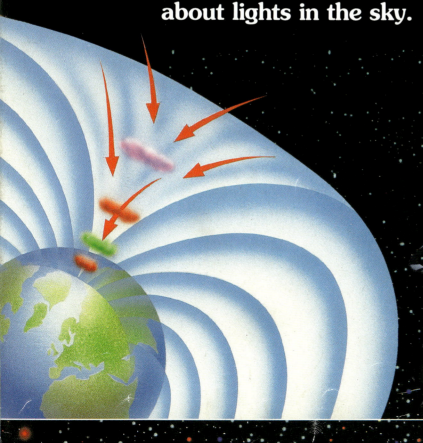

EXCELLENT EXPERIMENTS

Wherever you see this symbol (*below*), you'll find an experiment which you can do. Just follow the easy-to-understand instructions, and the results will open your eyes to the wonders of space. Find out why footprints stay on the Moon for millions of years and just how big the Solar System is.

OUR SOLAR SYSTEM

Look up into the night sky and the chances are that you'll see one or more of the planets. You can see up to five planets with the naked eye, and there are another three that can't be seen. These are too small or distant to be visible. With the Earth, this makes a total of nine planets, all of which orbit the Sun, which is the giant star of our Solar System.

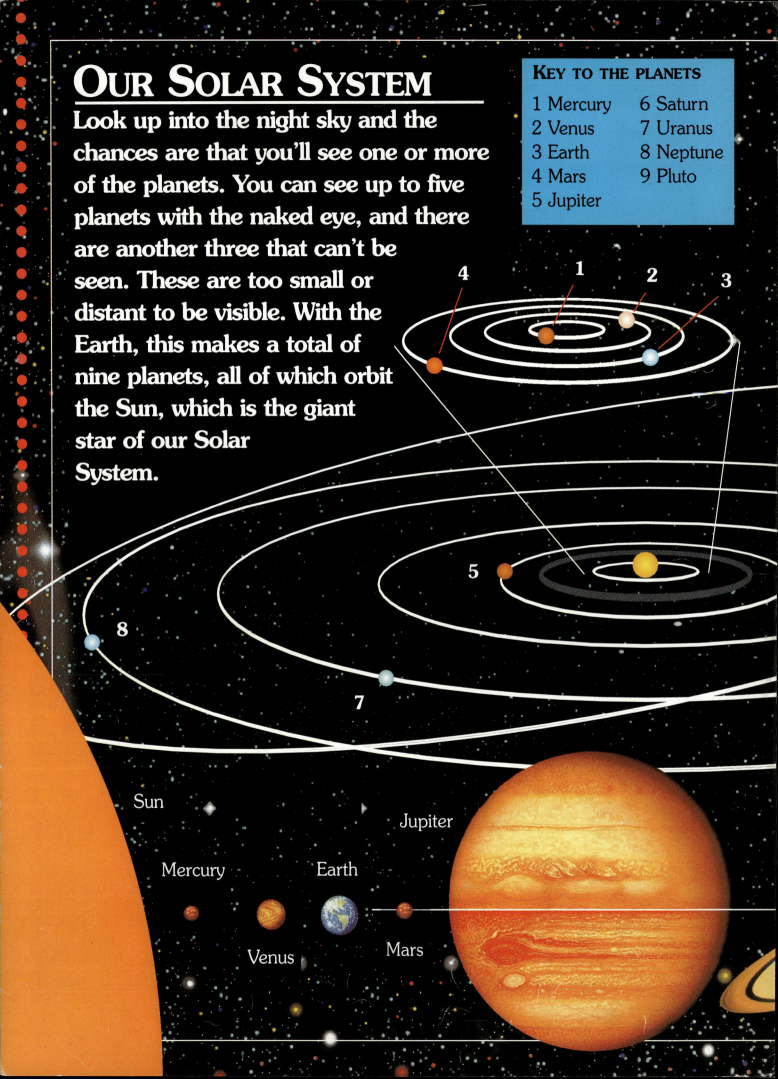

4

1

2

3

5

8

7

Sun

Jupiter

Mercury

Earth

Venus

Mars

BUILD YOUR OWN

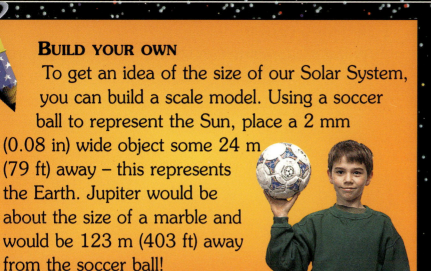

To get an idea of the size of our Solar System, you can build a scale model. Using a soccer ball to represent the Sun, place a 2 mm (0.08 in) wide object some 24 m (79 ft) away – this represents the Earth. Jupiter would be about the size of a marble and would be 123 m (403 ft) away from the soccer ball!

FACTS AND FIGURES

(a) DISTANCE FROM THE SUN
(b) WIDTH ACROSS EQUATOR

Mercury (a) 58 million km (36 million miles), (b) 4,880 km (3,030 miles)

Venus (a) 108 million km (67 million miles), (b) 12,105 km (7,520 miles)

Earth (a) 150 million km (93 million miles), (b) 12,820 km (7,960 miles)

Mars (a) 228 million km (142 million miles), (b) 6,790 km (4,220 miles)

Jupiter (a) 779 million km (484 million miles), (b) 143,042 km (88,890 miles)

Saturn (a) 1,428 million km (887 million miles), (b) 120,585 km (74,930 miles)

Uranus (a) 2,870 million km (1,780 million miles), (b) 51,140 km (31,780 miles)

Neptune (a) 4,500 million km (2,794 million miles), (b) 49,550 km (30,790 miles)

Pluto (a) 5,920 million km (3,675 million miles), (b) 2,285 km (1,419 miles)

9

6

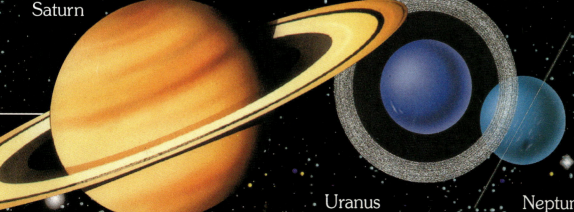

Saturn

Uranus

Neptune

Pluto

1 SPINNING CLOUD

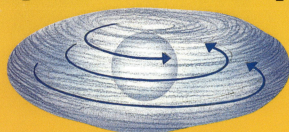

1

As the cloud started to shrink, it began to spin, forming itself into a disc (*left*). The area in the middle of the disc became the hottest part of the cloud, as the gas and dust particles were squeezed together by the cloud's gravity.

2

THE ORIGINS

Our Solar System is very, very old. Scientists believe it started out some 5 billion years ago as a huge clump of gas and dust that started to collapse in on itself, pulled together by gravity. As it got smaller, it began to get hotter in the middle, where much of the matter collected together. Eventually, this swirling cloud of dust formed the Sun and all of the planets.

2 HOT AND COLD

Deep inside the centre of the cloud, the temperature and pressure rose high enough to start nuclear fusion and our Sun began to shine (*above*).

3 BUILDING BLOCKS

The material in the disc around the new Sun clumped together to form bigger and bigger bodies. These bodies would later become the planets (*right*).

FALLING HISTORY

Meteorites (*left*), lumps of solid matter that have fallen from space onto the Earth's surface, tell us a great deal about the formation of the Solar System. Most meteorites are made of stone and some are made of metal or a mixture of stone and metal. Many of them date from the earliest days of the Solar System's formation.

OTHER STARS, OTHER SOLAR SYSTEMS
Astronomers can see clouds of gas and dust that are forming into new stars. They have also seen new stars with rings of matter around them (*left*), something like the ring of matter that was around our Sun from which the planets formed. They have even been able to detect some planets in orbit around other stars. From this, they believe that the formation of solar systems is not uncommon and that many stars have planets orbiting them. So far, the detected planets are all very large but scientists are working on ways of detecting smaller Earth-sized planets.

4 SYSTEM DEVELOPS
The major planets collected much of the matter in the Solar System. The outer planets quickly swept up the abundant ice and then attracted huge volumes of the gas hydrogen to become the four gas giants. The inner rocky worlds swept up the more dense rocks and metals to become Mercury, Venus, Earth and Mars (*below*).

3

4

MERCURY

Mercury is hard to spot from Earth. It orbits so close to the Sun that it is never far from it in the sky. The best times to catch a glimpse of it are at dawn and sunset. But never look for Mercury when the Sun is in the sky, as this can cause blindness!

Because Mercury is so close to the Sun, its surface temperature can reach 427°C. However, the temperature on the dark side of the planet can sink to -183°C. This is because Mercury has no atmosphere to keep it warm.

Pictures sent back by the Mariner 10 spacecraft show Mercury's surface to be very similar to our Moon's (below).

The Earth is over two and a half times wider than Mercury (left), *which is only 4,880 km (3,030 miles) across. In fact, Mercury is only a bit bigger than our Moon.*

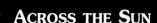

ACROSS THE SUN

Every so often Mercury passes across the face of the Sun when seen from Earth. When this happens, the tiny world is dwarfed by the Sun (*left*) – the Sun is nearly 300 times wider than Mercury. At its closest, Mercury is 46 million km (28 million miles) from the Sun and at its farthest, it is 70 million km (43 million miles) away.

MASSIVE CLIFFS

Areas of Mercury's surface are cut across by steep cliffs, known as scarps. Astronomers believe that these massive features may have been formed early in the planet's life when it was cooling and getting smaller.

One particular scarp, called Discovery Rupes (*right*), is over 500 km (310 miles) long. In some places, it stretches up 3 km (1.9 miles) above the surrounding surface. The area around it is pitted with craters.

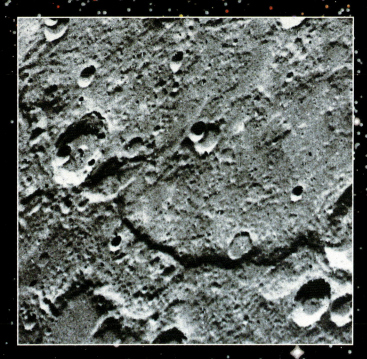

DEEP IMPACT

The lifeless surface of Mercury is almost completely covered with craters (*left*). Areas where there are larger craters alternate with regions of flat plains that are covered with smaller craters. The big craters are thought to be from impacts with huge chunks of matter and date from a few hundred million years after the planet was formed. One of these large craters, the Caloris Basin, is 1,300 km (807 miles) across. The small craters are from more recent impacts.

CRATER MAKER

You can make craters that look something like those on Mercury by dropping marbles into plaster of Paris. Fill a bowl with freshly mixed plaster of Paris and drop marbles into it. If the plaster is of the right consistency, it should form crater shapes like those on Mercury. When the plaster is hard, you've got your own cratered surface!

VENUS

Venus is more or less the same size and mass as the Earth and is not that much closer to the Sun than the Earth. What we see from Earth is a brightly shining, featureless world because all we can see are the clouds in its atmosphere. These clouds completely hide the surface below. Even spacecraft sent to look at Venus can't see down to its surface. Despite this, we know that Venus is an inhospitable place, with an atmosphere of carbon dioxide and a temperature of 465°C – hot enough to melt lead!

SHINING STAR

The third brightest object in the sky after the Sun and the Moon is the planet Venus (seen above the Moon, *left*). You can see Venus either before dawn or after sunset. Because of this, Venus is referred to as the Morning Star or the Evening Star.

IN A SWIRL

Images of Venus' clouds (*left*) show that they zoom around at speeds of about 350 km/h (217 mph), circling the planet once every four days. At one time it was thought that the planet rotated at the same rate. However, radar measurements of the planet's surface show that the planet rotates at a much slower speed. Beneath the clouds, the planet takes 243 days to rotate once on its axis. It also rotates in the opposite direction to all the other planets in the Solar System.

RADAR GLOBE

Visible light cannot reach us from the surface of Venus because of the planet's dense layer of clouds. But radar waves can reach down and bounce back. Radar mapping of the planet has revealed a world of low-lying plains, with occasional large impact craters. There are also two large highland regions (*below*).

PICTURES FROM THE SURFACE

This picture of Venus' surface (*above*) was sent back by the *Venera 13* probe which landed on the planet in 1982. On the surface, the probe encountered high temperatures, and pressures about 100 times those of Earth at sea-level!

COMPUTER MAP

This computer simulation, based on radar mapping, shows the region around Sapas Mons (*right*). This is a large volcano on Venus, about 400 km (248 miles) across and 1.5 km (0.9 miles) high.

LOOK AT THE PHASES

When the Sun is down, look at Venus through a small telescope (do not do it when the Sun is in the sky!). You'll probably see it as a slim crescent. Observe it over the course of several days and the size and shape of the crescent will change. However, because it orbits nearer to the Sun than the Earth does, you will never see Venus as a fully illuminated disc.

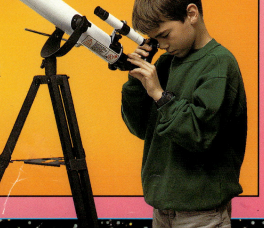

THE EARTH

As far as we know, there is no other part of the Solar System where there is life as we know it on Earth. The conditions on our planet are just right for life to have developed and for it to keep on evolving. The planet is alive in its own way, too. It has a hot interior and the solid-seeming crust on which we live floats on a layer of liquid rock below.

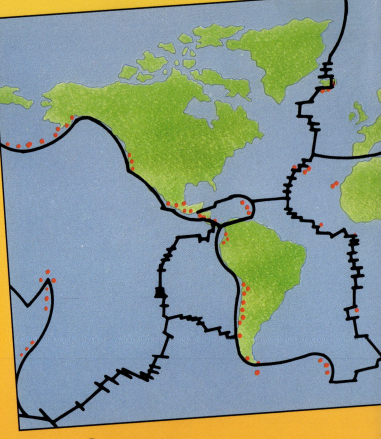

ON A PLATE

The Earth's crust is split into sections called plates. These plates are always being moved about by the liquid rock beneath. Where they rub against each other they can cause earthquakes and volcanic eruptions (red dots, *above*).

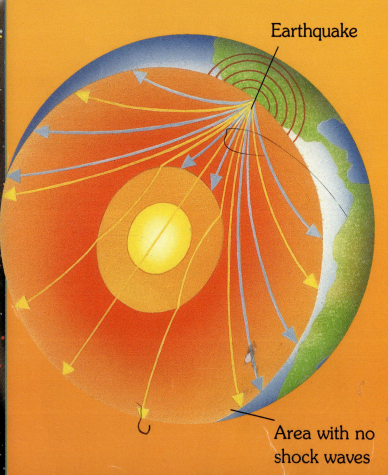

Earthquake

Area with no shock waves

SEEING INSIDE

When an earthquake occurs, it sends out shock waves which pass around and through the Earth. Scientists can use these shock waves to find out what lies towards the centre of our planet. For example, some shock waves are deflected by the change in density of the liquid rock found at the centre of the Earth (*left*). As a result, when they emerge on the other side of the Earth about 20 minutes later, there will be a ring-shaped area where none of these shock waves are recorded.

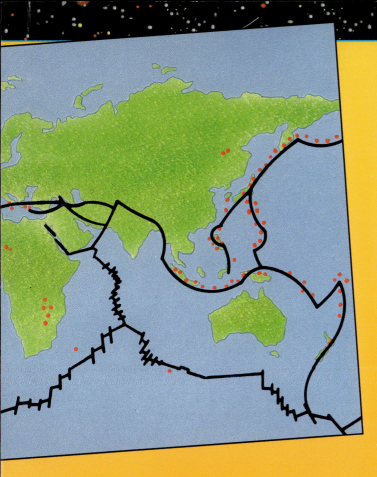

SHAKE UP

Where moving plates of the Earth's crust stick and do not slide past each other smoothly, they can store up energy and then release it in one sudden, large movement. This violent movement is called an earthquake. The damage from an earthquake can be extensive, flattening big cities (*above*) or causing huge tidal waves.

LIVING IN THE PAST

If you go out to collect fossils what you find is clear evidence that life has existed for a very long time – it takes millions of years for fossils to form. You may be able to find the fossils of sea-living creatures, such as ammonites (*below*), that are now lying out of the water. This is evidence that the Earth's plates are shifting, moving areas that were once under water to areas that are now dry ground.

LIT UP

From space, the signs that people live on Earth are not that obvious. At night, however, the major cities show up because of streetlighting and light from houses and factories. Here, the city of New York shows up clearly (*above*). To a visitor from space, this night-time light would be firm evidence that an advanced civilisation lived on Earth.

MARS

Mars, the next planet out from the Sun after the Earth, is smaller than the Earth, and because it is farther out, it gets less warmth from the Sun and is colder. Its average temperature is -55°C. Pictures taken by robot probes show mountains, plains, craters and signs that water has run on its surface at some time.

North Pole

South Pole

THE POLES

Like the Earth, Mars has two polar areas which are covered in ice (*above*). Like those on Earth, Mars' poles get bigger and smaller as the seasons change on the planet. However, Mars' polar ice-caps are made up mostly of frozen carbon dioxide, the gas that also makes up most of the planet's atmosphere.

PLANET MAPPING

Mars Global Surveyor (*right*) reached Mars in September 1997. Its continuing mission is to accurately map the entire surface of the planet. From its position in orbit around Mars, its highly accurate cameras will be able to see objects that are less than 1 m (3 ft) across – it may even be able to see the *Pathfinder* probe on the surface!

PATHFINDER

The *Pathfinder* probe (*below*) landed on Mars in July 1997. Cameras on the lander showed a dusty, barren plain scattered with stones and boulders. It also carried a small vehicle, called *Sojourner*, which left the probe to investigate rocks nearby.

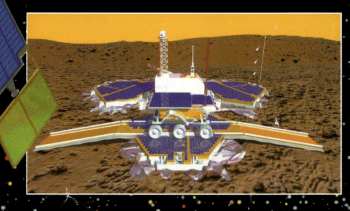

MIGHTY MOUNTAIN

Mars has the biggest volcano in the Solar System. Olympus Mons (*right*) is some 24 km (15 miles) high and nearly 540 km (335 miles) across its base. The crater at its summit is 90 km (56 miles) wide. Compare this with the largest active volcano on Earth, Mauna Loa in Hawaii. Shown below is the outline of Olympus Mons with the outline of the entire Hawaiian island chain in the foreground. Mauna Loa lies to the very right of this.

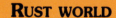

ANCIENT WATERS

Pictures taken by robot probes show features that look like water courses and erosion channels. It is thought that in the past, conditions occurred when liquid water could flow. It is not certain how these conditions could come about but the signs are clear. The atmosphere would have to be more dense and warmer for this to happen. Evidence points to these water-created features being nearly 4 billion years old.

RUST WORLD

When you look at Mars in the night sky, you will see that it is a dull red colour. You can find out why by trying a simple experiment. Take a new, ordinary iron or steel nail or key (it can't be stainless or galvanised). Leave it in a damp environment for a while and soon it will start to lose its shine and get a reddish coating. This is rust, and it is made when iron reacts with oxygen in the atmosphere to form iron oxide. Mars gets its reddish colour from iron oxide in the rocks and soil of its surface, but not from rusty keys!

JUPITER

Jupiter is the largest of the planets and can be the fourth brightest object in the sky. One reason it is so bright is that it's so big – it's about 11 times as wide as Earth – so it reflects a lot of the Sun's light. Jupiter is very different to Earth. Instead of being made mostly of rock, Jupiter is made mostly of the gases hydrogen and helium. It also has some faint rings.

Using infra-red telescopes, astronomers could 'see' the huge fireball that erupted when Shoemaker-Levy 9 *hit Jupiter's atmosphere (*left*).*

COMET CRASH

In July 1994, the fragments of a comet called *Shoemaker-Levy 9* collided with Jupiter. The comet had already been broken up into a chain of 21 fragments that stretched over 1 million km (620,000 miles). The Hubble Space Telescope showed huge 'holes' in the planet's atmosphere (*left*) where the fragments of the comet hit the planet. These holes were visible for up to a year after the impact, before they were erased by Jupiter's weather systems.

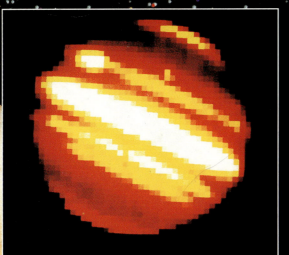

HOT INSIDE

Infra-red pictures of Jupiter show that it appears to be giving out heat (*left*). This heat is thought to come from the fact that the planet is slowly shrinking under the effect of its strong gravitational field. When gases are compressed, they heat up and it is this heat that can be 'seen'.

RED SPOT

One feature you can spot with a small telescope is Jupiter's Great Red Spot (*right*). This is a huge storm in the southern hemisphere of the planet. It is three times wider than the Earth! The spot has been visible to astronomers for well over 300 years.

SWIRLING CLOUDS

You can make a pattern on paper something like the bands on Jupiter. Fill a shallow tray with some water. Then, with an adult's help, pour some liquid oil paints of different colours onto the water – the paints should float on top of the water. Move a pointer across the floating paints in a series of parallel lines to form the bands. Then put a sheet of paper on the top of the water so that it picks up the paints on the surface. Lift out the paper and dry it. The parallel lines on the paper will look like Jupiter's bands.

BANDED PLANET

Pictures taken by space probes show Jupiter's surface to be made up of bands of clouds (*above*). You might be able to see these bands using a telescope. These clouds are made of different chemicals, including ammonia and water crystals.

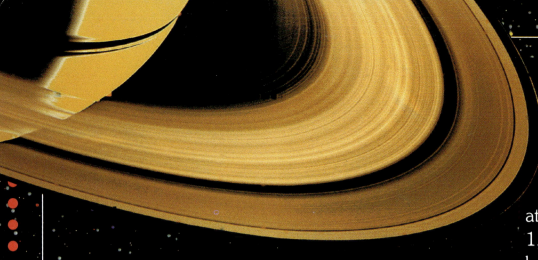

Astronomers calculate that there are probably 10,000 or more ringlets (*left*). The rings are not very thick, at only between 30 and 1,000 m (98 to 3,280 ft) broad, and they are not solid but made up of small particles (*see right*). The rings start some 7,000 km (4,350 miles) above Saturn's clouds, and stretch out to 74,000 km (46,000 miles) above the clouds.

SATURN

One of the most extraordinary sights of the Solar System is the planet Saturn. Look at it through a small telescope and you will almost certainly see at least one ring around it, possibly two. In pictures from space probes, we can see that these big rings are, in fact, thousands of tiny ringlets.

2009

2005

2000

1995

SURFACE OF THE GIANT

Like Jupiter, Saturn's surface is patterned in bands (*left*). Although Saturn does not have a startling feature like Jupiter's Great Red Spot, it does have storms of its own in the form of white spots, brown spots and a red oval. Below its clouds, the gases are squashed into liquid. Right at the centre is a rocky core.

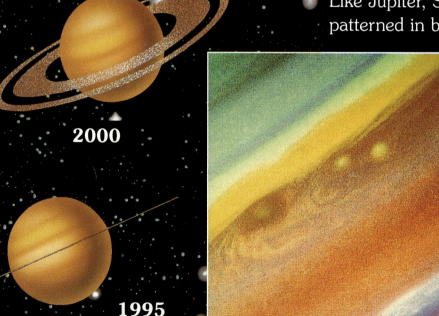

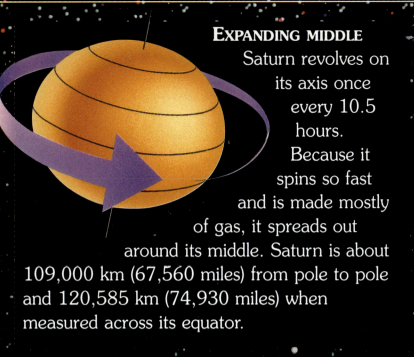

EXPANDING MIDDLE

Saturn revolves on its axis once every 10.5 hours. Because it spins so fast and is made mostly of gas, it spreads out around its middle. Saturn is about 109,000 km (67,560 miles) from pole to pole and 120,585 km (74,930 miles) when measured across its equator.

CHANGING RINGS

Watch Saturn's rings over the course of a few years and you'll notice that they seem to open and close. This is because Saturn is tilted at an angle of 25° to the plane of its orbit, and so are its rings. As we see them from the Earth, which orbits much closer to the Sun, we see the rings open, close and open again over the course of about 30 years as Saturn completes its orbit around the Sun which lasts 29.5 years (see dates and orientations, *left*).

2011

2016

2021

INSIDE THE RINGS

The rings are made of countless particles (*below*) ranging in size from minute particles, to snowflakes, up to chunks the size of large boulders. Although no pictures have been taken of individual particles, they are thought to be made mostly of ice with some dust and possibly some metallic material.

Astronomers have seen that some of the rings appear to be twisted together. It is thought that this 'braiding' has been caused by small 'shepherd' moons which orbit on either side of the twisted rings. As the moons pass by, their gravitational field distorts the rings.

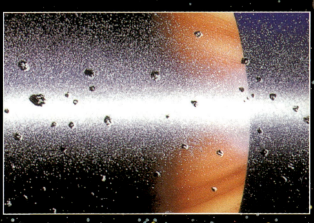

URANUS

Although it is the third largest planet in the Solar System, Uranus is almost impossible to see with the naked eye because it is so far away from us. Like Jupiter and Saturn, it's made mostly of the gases hydrogen and helium with some methane. The methane gives the planet its bluish colour when it is looked at through a powerful telescope.

FEATURELESS PLANET

When probes look at the planet it seems fairly featureless (*above*). However, if looked at in infra-red it shows banded clouds and weather systems like those of Jupiter.

DISCOVERING RINGS

Uranus' rings cannot be seen from Earth, but they can be detected. When the rings pass in front of a star, the light levels from the star change, almost seeming to flicker (*right*). This 'flickering' can be picked up with instruments that measure light levels. There are nine rings in all (*left*) and they are made of some of the darkest matter in the Solar System. They start some 16,000 km (9,940 miles) above the planet and extend for 10,000 km (6,210 miles).

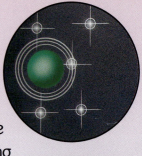
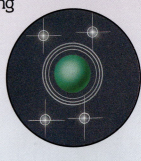
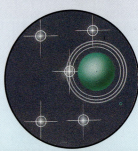

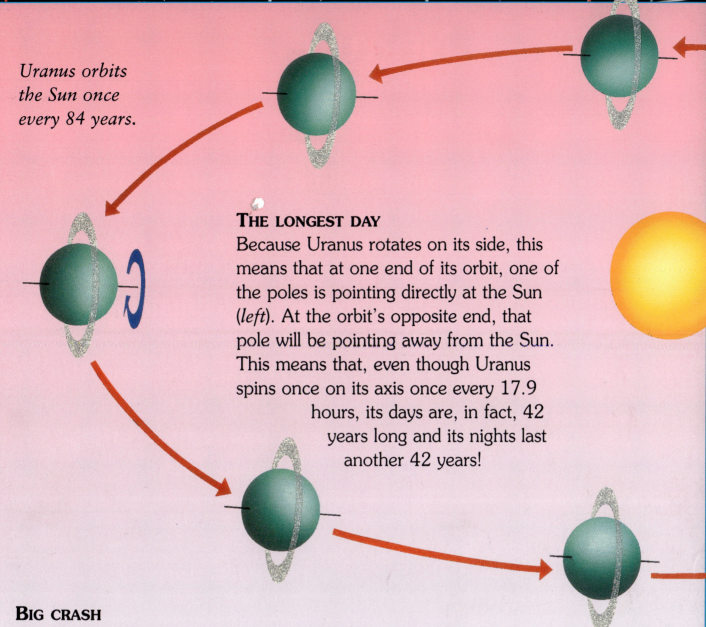

Uranus orbits the Sun once every 84 years.

THE LONGEST DAY

Because Uranus rotates on its side, this means that at one end of its orbit, one of the poles is pointing directly at the Sun (*left*). At the orbit's opposite end, that pole will be pointing away from the Sun. This means that, even though Uranus spins once on its axis once every 17.9 hours, its days are, in fact, 42 years long and its nights last another 42 years!

BIG CRASH

The planets all spin at a tilt to the plane of their orbits – the Earth tilts at 23.5°. But Uranus is unique in that it is tilted more than any other, at an angle of 98° – it actually spins on its side in relation to its orbit around the Sun (*see above*)!

Astronomers are not certain why Uranus is so tilted, but one theory is that at some time the planet suffered a colossal impact, one powerful enough to literally knock it sideways (*right*). To do this, the object would have had to have been at least half the size of the Earth, about 6,400 km (4,000 miles) across, compared with Uranus' own diameter of 51,140 km (31,780 miles).

NEPTUNE

Neptune is the last of the four giant gas planets. Due to Pluto's strange orbit (*see* pages 24-25), Neptune can sometimes be the farthest planet from the Sun. Because it's so far away, it's too faint to see with the naked eye. Like Uranus, Neptune has an atmosphere containing some methane, making the planet appear a bluish colour. It does, however, have a few features that Uranus lacks.

When the robot probe Voyager visited Neptune, it saw a large feature that was given the name the Great Dark Spot (above). However, when the Hubble Space Telescope looked at Neptune in 1994, this feature seemed to have disappeared.

NEPTUNE'S RINGS

Neptune has four, thin rings (*right*) that are very dim, like those of Jupiter and Uranus. The outermost ring has sections of it which seem brighter than the rest.

HIGH-FLYING CLOUDS

Small, white clouds, probably methane ice crystals, drift high in the atmosphere of blue Neptune, floating some 50 km (31 miles) above the blue cloud deck (*left*).

Despite seeming calm, Neptune is home to some very strong winds and storms which rage across its surface. In fact, it is thought to have the strongest winds in the Solar System – the fastest winds blow at about 2,000 km/h (1,250 mph).

SCOOTER

Another feature is called the Scooter (*right*). This white cloud zooms around the planet once every 16.8 hours.

BLUE PLANET

Voyager's pictures from close-up reveal faint banding in the clouds of the planet (*right*). As well as the high methane clouds, there are lower cloud layers of ammonia and hydrogen sulphide. These blue lower layers are what we see when astronomers look at the planet.

LESS DENSE

On Earth, the gases hydrogen and helium are lighter than our atmosphere – you can see this when a helium-filled balloon rises into the air. The giant gas planets (Jupiter, Saturn, Uranus and Neptune) are made up mostly of these gases. Because these gases are so light, these gassy planets are not as dense as the rocky planets, such as The Earth.

PLUTO AND CHARON

After the gas giants, Pluto is a real change – it's tiny. Earth is five times wider and is 500 times as massive. Because Pluto is so distant and so small, it has been hard for astronomers to get to know it. Nevertheless, it is thought that Pluto has a rocky core covered with a deep layer of water-ice, on top of which is a mixed layer of frozen methane and ice.

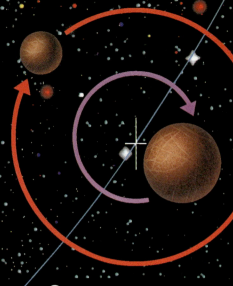

CLOSE ORBIT

Pluto has a moon called Charon. Charon orbits Pluto very closely, making Pluto and Charon a double planet. Charon is 20 times closer to Pluto than the Moon is to the Earth. As they orbit each other, they both seem to loop along their orbit around the Sun because the centre of gravity of the two planets is outside of Pluto (*above*).

Charon

Pluto

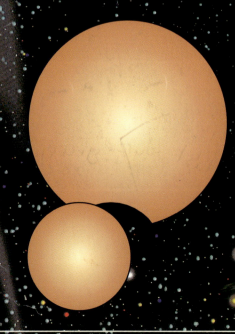

CHANGING BRIGHTNESS

As Pluto and Charon orbit each other, they sometimes pass in front of or behind each other. Using equipment similar to that used to discover Uranus' rings (*see* page 20), astronomers have observed how the light given out by the two bodies changes when they do this. They have found that the light from the planets is much dimmer when Charon passes across Pluto than when Pluto passes in front of Charon. This is due to Charon's shadow passing over Pluto and the fact that Charon's surface is darker than Pluto's (*above*).

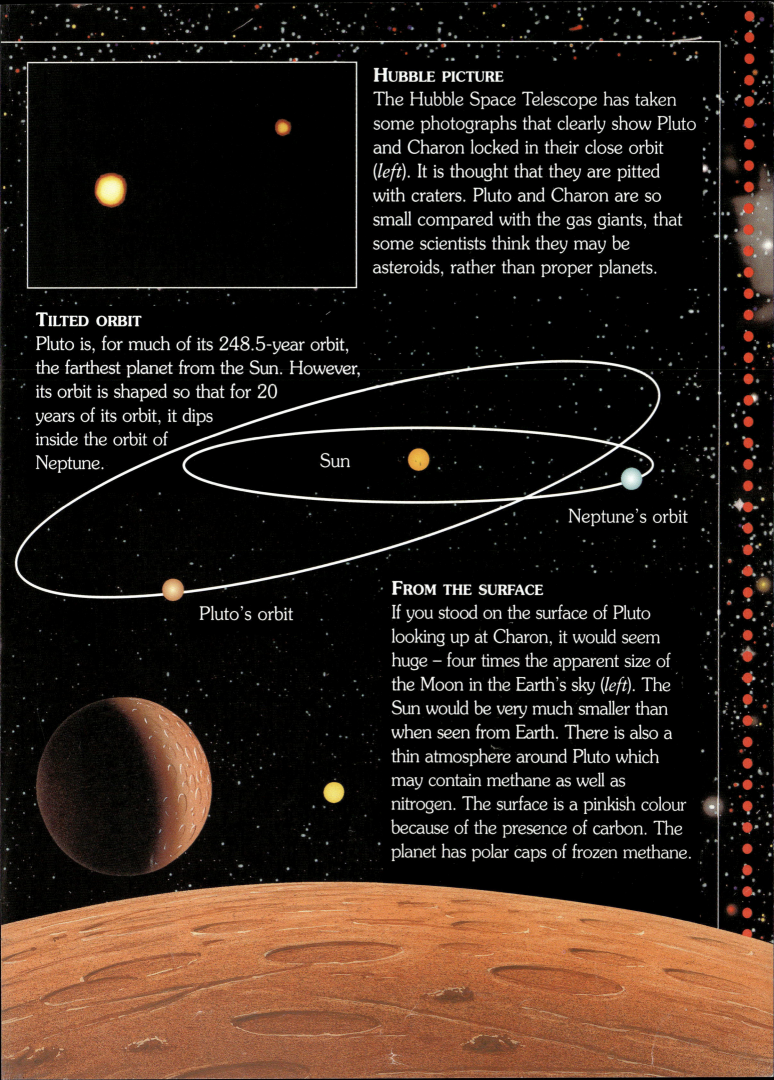

HUBBLE PICTURE

The Hubble Space Telescope has taken some photographs that clearly show Pluto and Charon locked in their close orbit (*left*). It is thought that they are pitted with craters. Pluto and Charon are so small compared with the gas giants, that some scientists think they may be asteroids, rather than proper planets.

TILTED ORBIT

Pluto is, for much of its 248.5-year orbit, the farthest planet from the Sun. However, its orbit is shaped so that for 20 years of its orbit, it dips inside the orbit of Neptune.

Sun

Neptune's orbit

Pluto's orbit

FROM THE SURFACE

If you stood on the surface of Pluto looking up at Charon, it would seem huge – four times the apparent size of the Moon in the Earth's sky (*left*). The Sun would be very much smaller than when seen from Earth. There is also a thin atmosphere around Pluto which may contain methane as well as nitrogen. The surface is a pinkish colour because of the presence of carbon. The planet has polar caps of frozen methane.

ASTEROIDS

There are countless chunks of rocks and ice in our Solar System, much of them left over from the time when it formed. Most of these fragments are called asteroids and many of these asteroids orbit the Sun between Mars and Jupiter. You cannot see any of them with the naked eye, but some of the larger ones are visible with good binoculars or a small telescope.

ODD-SHAPED ROCKS

As this picture of the asteroid Ida shows (*below*), asteroids can come in odd shapes. Although some are round, many are stretched out or have completely random shapes.

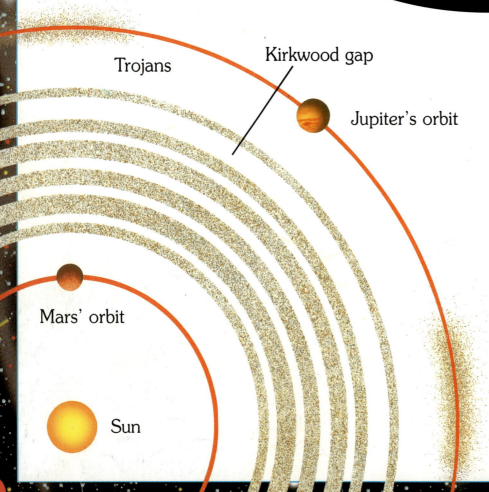

Trojans

Kirkwood gap

Jupiter's orbit

Mars' orbit

Sun

ASTEROIDS IN ORBIT

Most asteroids orbit the Sun between Mars and Jupiter, some 300 to 600 million km (186 to 372 million miles) out from the Sun (*left*). In this so-called Asteroid Belt are regions where there are relatively less asteroids. These are called Kirkwood gaps after their discoverer, the American astronomer Daniel Kirkwood. There are also two groups of asteroids that orbit at the same distance as Jupiter, called the Trojans.

ON THE TRAIL

Asteroids are very difficult to see because they are very small and very dark. You need very sensitive equipment to capture the movement of an asteroid across the sky. Asteroids normally show up on photographs or on electronically captured images as trails across the stationary background stars (blue trail, *right*). By looking at the trail, astronomers can work out the orbit of the asteroid and gain information about its size.

CERES

The largest known asteroid is called Ceres. It is some 933 km (579 miles) across, about as wide as the state of Texas, USA (*below*). In fact, Ceres is estimated to contain as much as one quarter to one third of the total mass of the asteroids. Astronomers have discovered some 7,000 asteroids and many more are being found every month. There are only 26 asteroids that are wider than 200 km (124 miles), and astronomers have found almost all those that are greater than 100 km (62 miles) across.

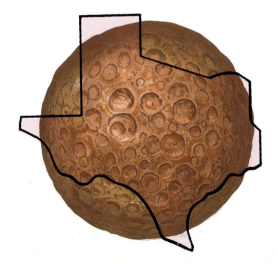

BIG HIT

As well as the Trojans and those asteroids in the Asteroid Belt, there are a number of asteroids that cross the Earth's orbit. Like other planets, the Earth carries the scars of several impacts with other bodies (*below*). One example includes a massive crater off the coast of Mexico. The impact which created this may have wiped out the dinosaurs.

During its close encounter with Halley's comet, Giotto sent back pictures of the comet's nucleus. This picture (right) shows the nucleus throwing off jets of gas and dust that are being boiled off by the Sun.

Gas tail

COMETS

Comets are small, icy bodies with long, streaming tails which orbit the Sun. You can watch their tails grow over the space of a few weeks as they approach the Sun, and then fade as they go back out into space. Many comets return at regular intervals. The orbit of Halley's comet means that it returns roughly every 76 years.

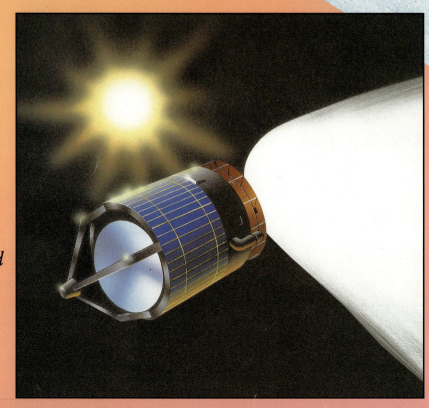

When Halley's comet approached the Sun in 1986, several probes were sent to investigate it. One, called Giotto (right), flew to within 596 km (370 miles) of the comet's nucleus.

Solar System

BEYOND THE SOLAR SYSTEM

Astronomers believe that comets come from a region of space outside the Solar System, called the Oort cloud (*left*). It is thought that the Oort cloud could contain some 100 billion cometary bodies, separated from each other by many millions of kilometres. These bodies are deflected by chance collisions with each other, or by the gravity of a passing star, and hurtle towards the Sun. When they move towards the Sun, they fall into a very long, stretched-out orbit that can take thousands of years to complete.

Oort cloud

Dust tail

Layers of ice and dust

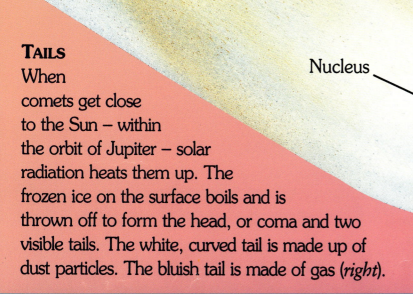

Nucleus

Solar radiation

TAILS

When comets get close to the Sun – within the orbit of Jupiter – solar radiation heats them up. The frozen ice on the surface boils and is thrown off to form the head, or coma and two visible tails. The white, curved tail is made up of dust particles. The bluish tail is made of gas (*right*).

THE MOON

When you look at the Moon you see a few blurry features on a bright silver disc. But no matter how hard you look, you'll only ever see one side of the Moon. This is because it takes the same amount of time for the Moon to spin once on its axis as it does to perform one orbit around the Earth.

THE MOON'S FACE

The Moon's landscape is covered in craters and darker areas called mare (from the Latin for 'sea', *right*). Mare are huge plains where lava has welled up from beneath and covered the features of the surface.

EXPLORING THE MOON

Between 1969 and 1972, six Apollo spacecraft carried astronauts to the Moon (*left*). In total, 12 men actually walked on the Moon. However, more information has been found by robot probes. Most recently, one probe found evidence that there is water on the Moon, hidden in craters at the poles where sunshine cannot get at it.

THAT'S ONE SMALL FOOTPRINT

Make a footprint in some sand outside and watch it over the course of a few days or weeks. When it rains and when the wind blows, the footprint starts to become indistinct and eventually completely vanishes. On the Moon, the footprints left in the soil by the Apollo astronauts (*above*) will not be obliterated for millions of years because there is no atmosphere to speak of, and therefore no weather.

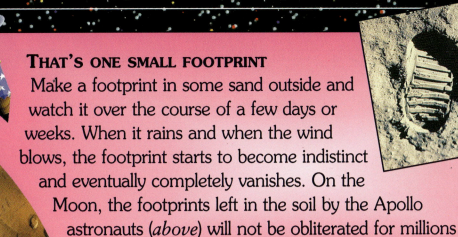

MOON MAKER

There are three main theories as to how the Moon formed where it did, so close to the Earth. In the first, the Moon formed from the debris which resulted from a huge impact on the Earth (*see above right*).

In the second, it formed separately and at the same time as the Earth. It would have formed from a disc of debris around the Earth, much like the planets formed around the Sun when the Solar System was taking shape.

In the third theory, the Moon is thought to have formed somewhere else in the Solar System, before being captured later by the Earth's gravitational field. However, this theory is extremely unlikely.

The most widely accepted theory for the formation involves an impact by a large object (1). This sent debris up into orbit (2), which then clumped together to form the Moon (3).

1

2

3

SATELLITES

With the naked eye, the only natural satellite of a planet you can see is the Moon, orbiting the Earth. But many of the Solar System's planets have satellites of their own – only Mercury and Venus have none. Some of these moons are just tiny chunks of rock, little more than asteroids. Others are worlds in their own right, and some have conditions which could harbour primitive forms of life.

THE MOON

At 3,476 km (2,159 miles) across, our Moon (*above*) is one of the larger moons in the Solar System (*see right*). It is the Earth's closest companion in space, and being so nearby, has offered us a different world to study and explore more or less on our doorstep.

Mimas

Callisto

Dione

JUPITER'S MOONS

Jupiter has at least 16 moons. Of these, the four largest (Io, Europa, Ganymede and Callisto) are called the Galilean satellites after the astronomer Galileo who first saw them in 1610. Ganymede (*left*) is icy with a surface pitted with craters. Callisto (*above left*) has a crater-scarred surface. Europa (*above right*) has a smooth surface of ice with liquid water, beneath which might harbour life. The surface of Io is scarred by volcanoes (*see right*).

SATURN'S SATELLITES

Saturn has more than 20 satellites, including Dione and Mimas (*left* and *above*). Mimas is a small, icy moon with many craters, one of which is 130 km (81 miles) across – nearly one-third of the moon's diameter! Dione's surface is covered in large streaks. Another of Saturn's moons, Titan, has an atmosphere which consists mostly of nitrogen, argon and methane.

PHOBOS AND DEIMOS

Mars has a couple of small satellites, Phobos and Deimos (*right*). Phobos is the larger at 27 km (17 miles) long and Deimos is 15 km (9 miles) long. They are irregularly shaped lumps of cratered rock, possibly asteroids captured by Mars' gravity. They both orbit quite close to Mars and travel very quickly, rising and setting twice each Martian day.

Phobos

Deimos

Europa

Io

THE 35 BIGGEST MOONS	
Moon (Planet)	Diameter (km)
Ganymede (Jupiter)	5,268
Titan (Saturn)	5,150
Callisto (Jupiter)	4,806
Io (Jupiter)	3,642
Moon (Earth)	3,476
Europa (Jupiter)	3,130
Triton (Neptune)	2,706
Titania (Uranus)	1,578
Rhea (Saturn)	1,528
Oberon (Uranus)	1,522
Iapetus (Saturn)	1,436
Charon (Pluto)	1,172
Umbriel (Uranus)	1,170
Ariel (Uranus)	1,162
Dione (Saturn)	1,120
Tethys (Saturn)	1,060
Enceladus (Saturn)	498
Miranda (Uranus)	472
Proteus (Neptune)	418
Mimas (Saturn)	398
Nereid (Neptune)	340
Hyperion (Saturn)	286
Phoebe (Saturn)	220
Larissa (Neptune)	192
Amalthea (Jupiter)	188
Himalia (Jupiter)	186
Galatea (Neptune)	158
Puck (Uranus)	154
Despina (Neptune)	148
Sycorax (Uranus)	120
Epimetheus (Saturn)	114
Janus (Saturn)	114
Portia (Uranus)	110
Thebe (Jupiter)	100
Prometheus (Saturn)	92

ERUPTIONS ON IO

When the *Voyager 2* space probe passed Io in 1979, it made an astonishing discovery. Plumes of material (*right*) were being shot out from the planet's surface up to an altitude of 300 km (186 miles). It was the first evidence of active volcanoes on another body other than the Earth. Astronomers have dubbed the moon the most volcanic body in the Solar System.

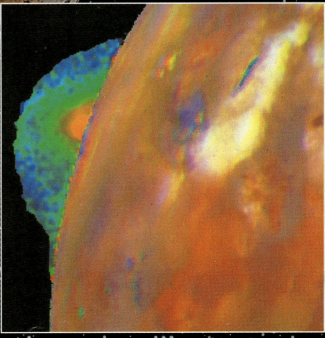

AURORAE AND MAGNETOSPHERES

Deep below your feet, a huge dynamo is generating electric currents that have the effect of creating a powerful magnetic field. This is the Earth's magnetic field and it is easy to detect – just look at a compass which points north. Other planets also have magnetic fields and some of these have an effect over many millions of miles.

DYNAMO EARTH

The Earth's magnetic field is made deep below the surface, in the molten parts of our planet's hot iron core. In this region, eddies in the liquid metal create electric currents, a bit like in a dynamo, which in turn generate a magnetic field (*above*).

Coloured lights

SKY LIGHTS

The Earth's magnetic field makes a good shield against the particles that shoot out from the Sun, the solar wind. Only at the poles can these particles get close to the Earth. When they hit the atmosphere, they can make gases in the atmosphere glow, creating displays of colour called aurorae. Different gases glow at different heights with different colours. At about 1,000 km (620 miles) nitrogen can glow violet, while at about 300 km (186 miles) oxygen can glow red (*left*).

MIGHTY MAGNETOSPHERE

Jupiter has the most powerful magnetic field of all the planets. It is generated by electric currents that flow in the layers deep within the planet, where hydrogen behaves like a liquid metal. The magnetic field of Jupiter is between 10 and 30 times stronger than the Earth's. This powerful field is called the magnetosphere (*right*). On the side of the field facing the Sun, it deflects the particles shot out by the Sun (the solar wind) and is compressed. Away from the Sun, the solar wind blows the magnetosphere out into a long tail. This tail is so long that it could stretch as far out as the orbit of Saturn.

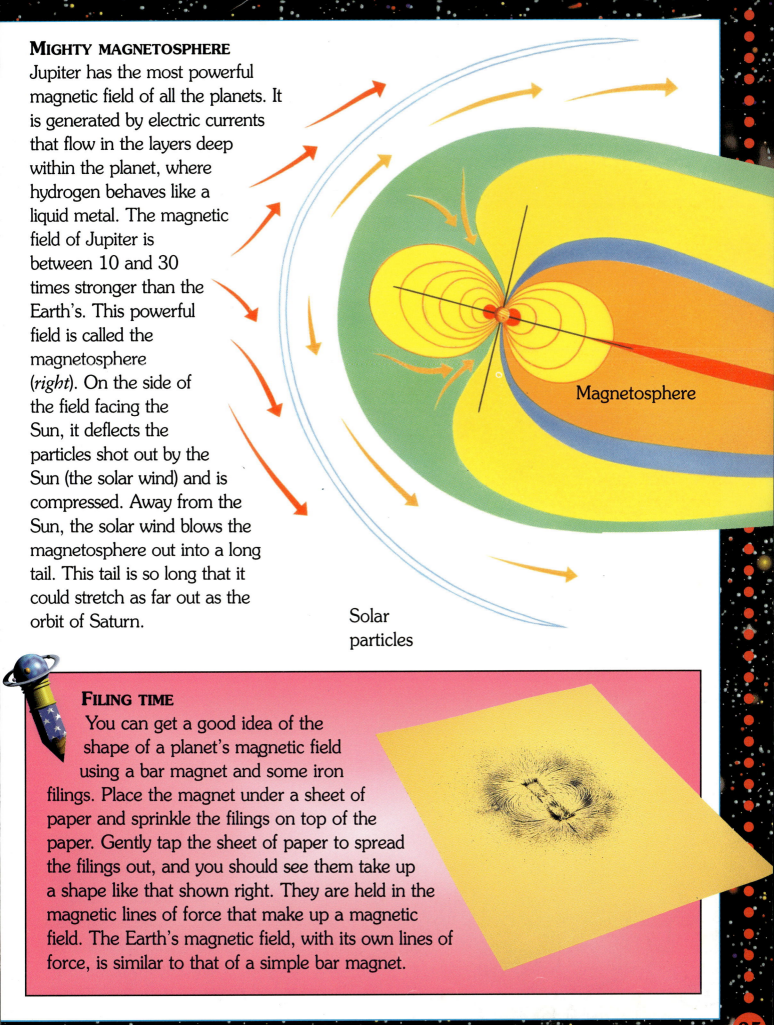

Magnetosphere

Solar particles

FILING TIME

You can get a good idea of the shape of a planet's magnetic field using a bar magnet and some iron filings. Place the magnet under a sheet of paper and sprinkle the filings on top of the paper. Gently tap the sheet of paper to spread the filings out, and you should see them take up a shape like that shown right. They are held in the magnetic lines of force that make up a magnetic field. The Earth's magnetic field, with its own lines of force, is similar to that of a simple bar magnet.

WEATHER ON THE PLANETS

All the worlds that have substantial atmospheres have weather. Because we live on it, we know more about the Earth's weather than that on any other planet or moon. All you have to do is look outside to see the weather in action. However, even our most powerful and destructive weather patterns seem puny when compared with some of the storms that rage in the Solar System.

Every so often, Mars suffers massive storms when the whole surface can be hidden by dust in the atmosphere (arrowed above).

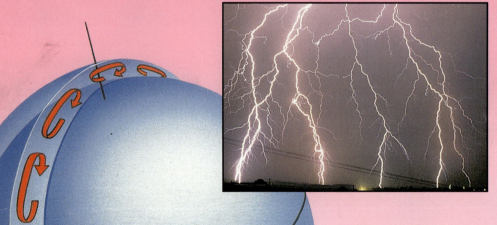

Lightning (left) does not only appear on the Earth. Jupiter, for instance, has extremely powerful lightning bolts which flash frequently in its atmosphere.

SPREADING THE HEAT

The weather on Earth, and on all the other planets, is caused by a redistribution of energy. In the case of the Earth, this involves the movement of heat away from the Equator. This is generally achieved by three air currents in each hemisphere (*left*). These move hot air up and outwards from warmer regions and replace it with cooler air.

BIG CHILL

It can get very cold on Earth – the coldest temperatures recorded are around -85°C. But such extremes are only found in polar regions. Over most of the Earth the temperature is above freezing almost all the time and the Earth's overall average temperature is a mild 15°C. The coldest place in the Solar System is on Neptune's moon Triton, where it measures a chilly -235°C!

A storm in the tropics can cause a lot of damage (right). The fastest winds on Earth can reach 450 km/h (280 mph). The strongest winds in the Solar System are thought to be on Neptune, where they can blow at 2,000 km/h (1,250 mph).

WEATHER WATCH

It would be very difficult for you to keep track of the weather on other planets, although you can see Jupiter's Great Red Spot storm with a telescope. However, you can record the Earth's weather conditions with a few simple items of equipment. With a thermometer, record the temperature at fixed times every day and keep a chart to show how the temperature varies over the course of a year. You can make a rainfall gauge by cutting off the top of a plastic bottle and turning the top upside down, before sticking it back onto the bottle. Add a scale to the side of the bottle and see how much rain has fallen every day, and keep a record.

GLOSSARY

Asteroids
Small, rocky objects, the greatest collection of which orbit the Sun in a band called the Asteroid Belt between Mars and Jupiter.

Atmosphere
The layer of gases which surround a planet. The atmosphere around the Earth supplies us with the gases which keep us alive.

Aurorae
Multi-coloured lights that appear in the skies above the North and South Poles. When charged particles sent out by the Sun (the solar wind) arrive at the Earth, they are funnelled by the Earth's magnetic field into the atmosphere above the Poles. When these particles enter the atmosphere, they react with the air to create the lights.

Comets
Lumps of ice and dust which orbit the Sun. As a comet approaches the Sun, radiation from the Sun causes the ice and dust to boil off, creating huge tails which stretch out behind the comet.

Compass
A device which can detect a planet's magnetic field using a magnetised needle.

Day
The length of time it takes for a planet to complete one rotation. An Earth day lasts 23.93 hours, while a day on Saturn lasts only 10.23 hours.

Double planet
Instead of having one small moon orbiting around a planet, a double planet has two similar-sized objects orbiting around each other.

Earthquake
The Earth's surface is made up of plates. When two of these plates rub against each other they cause a violent upheaval which is known as an earthquake.

Equator
An imaginary line which runs around a planet at an equal distance from its two poles. It marks the planet's widest part.

Gravity
Every object in the Universe has a force which attracts it to every other object. This force is called gravity. The larger or more dense the object, the greater its gravitational force. A large and very dense object, such as the Sun, will have a higher gravitational force than a smaller, less dense object, such as a planet like the Earth.

Meteors

Objects which hit the Earth's atmosphere and burn up leaving a fiery trail which disappears after a few seconds. Objects which hit the Earth's surface are called meteorites.

Moons

Small bodies which orbit around some of the major planets. The Earth has one moon, while Venus has none and Jupiter has at least 16!

Oort cloud

A region of space beyond the orbit of Pluto, the Oort cloud contains billions of icy bodies that may become comets.

Orbit

The path of an object, such as a planet or a comet, around another object, such as a star.

Planets

Large objects which orbit around a star. These can be rocky planets such as the Earth, Venus or Mars, or gassy giant planets, such as Jupiter, Uranus or Saturn.

Pole

A point on a planet's surface around which the planet spins, or rotates.

Rings

The larger, gas planets are surrounded by rings. These rings are not solid, but are made up from millions of particles.

Satellite

An object which goes around another, larger object. Satellites can be natural, such as moons, or artificial, such as weather satellites.

Solar System

The group of major planets, including the Earth, and minor planets which orbit the Sun.

Telescope

A device which magnifies (makes bigger) an object that is being looked at. Astronomers use telescopes to look at the stars and the planets. Telescopes can collect visible light or they can catch invisible radiation, including radio waves and infra-red radiation.

Volcano

An opening in a planet's crust through which molten rock or chemicals can gush. The largest volcano in the Solar System is found on Mars and is called Olympus Mons.

INDEX

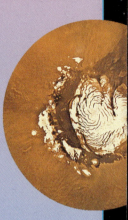